How To Be I

Lessons from Paul

Mike Breen
Senior Pastor, Community Church of Joy, Arizona
Formerly Rector, St Thomas' Crookes, Sheffield

Ian Paul
Dean of Studies, St John's College, Nottingham
Managing Editor, Grove Books Ltd

GROVE BOOKS LIMITED
RIDLEY HALL RD CAMBRIDGE CB3 9HU

Contents

'Without me you can do nothing...I appointed you to bear much fruit, fruit that will last.'
(John 15.5, 8, 16)

Mike Breen delivered the core of this material in two talks as part of the seminar programme
at New Wine in the summer of 2004.
Ian Paul transcribed the talks, added framing material and edited it into its current form.

The Cover Illustration is by Peter Ashton

Copyright © Mike Breen, Ian Paul 2005
Bible quotations are taken from the New International Version
© 1973, 1978, 1984 International Bible Society

First Impression April 2005
ISSN 1470-8531
ISBN 1 85174 591 2

Introduction

1

In the Western church, there is a deep anxiety about the success or otherwise of our ministry.

In the UK, constantly declining church attendance figures have forced us to ask some hard questions about ourselves and about our understanding of what Jesus has called us to be and do. But even in places where there appears to be success, people continue to ask questions about whether they have got it right. The quest for success can simply lead us to a series of effective techniques, and deep down we know that this is not what matters. What matters—what Jesus longs for us and can give us—is fruitfulness.

In this booklet we are going to look at Paul and his ministry in relation to two of the cities that he visited, Philippi and Corinth, places he visited as part of his second missionary journey when he ventured into Europe for the first time. No follower of Jesus has been as fruitful as Paul, because no follower of Jesus has been as faithful as Paul in following in the steps of his master.

Discussions about ministry and about fruitfulness have often, in the past, focussed on one area or another of life in ministry. Some (for example, the church growth movement) have tended to focus on outward things—questions of strategy or technique. Others (for example, those looking at the nature of leadership) have focussed on the hidden questions of the leader's inner life.

But our insights into Paul's ministry come not only from the account of what he did, in the Acts of the Apostles, but also from Paul's own account of what he thought, in this case in his letters to the Christians at Corinth. We have access not only to a record of the actions of Paul but also a record of how he reflected on those actions and shared that reflection with others. As a result, Paul can teach us about both the outer aspects of fruitfulness, which has to do with strategy, and also inner aspects of fruitfulness, the secret of the fruitful heart.

Paul can teach us about both the outer and also inner aspects of fruitfulness

This offers us a uniquely powerful insight into the fruitfulness of this most fruitful of disciples. We will look at these two aspects, the outer and the inner, in turn as we consider his ministry in these two cities of Philippi and Corinth.

2   Part 1:
 The Strategy for Fruitfulness

The account of Paul's ministry in the Acts of the Apostles centres on two periods of itinerant ministry, often called Paul's first and secondary missionary journeys. (You can find maps of these journeys at the back of most Bibles.) The persecution of the church in Jerusalem has driven the followers of Jesus to other cities where they share the Good News with Gentiles as well as Jews, and following Peter's realization in Acts 10 that the message about Jesus the Messiah is for all, these new mixed communites thrive and grow. This is the first wave of the movement of the gospel beyond Jerusalem and Judea and Samaria as predicted by Jesus in Acts 1 before his Ascension.

It is Paul's missionary journeys which are the main impetus behind the next waves of the gospel reaching further around the Mediterranean basin, and into Europe itself. This is a period of rapid growth for the church; in city after city, new Christian communities come into being. What is it that makes Paul so effective as a leader in this growth?

Step 1: Recognize the Time

We pick up the story of Paul's travels near the beginning of his second missionary journey in Acts 16.

> Paul and his companions travelled throughout the region of Phrygia and Galatia, having been kept by the Holy Spirit from preaching the word in the province of Asia. When they came to the border of Mysia, they tried to enter Bithynia, but the Spirit of Jesus would not allow them to. So they passed by Mysia and went down to Troas.   (Acts 16.6–8)

Paul is going through what some would call 'dog's leg guidance'; it is not a straight road, but is an experience which will bring big changes for Paul. He wants to go to Asia, which is in the south-west region of Galatia and Phrygia, but the Lord would not let him. So instead, he attempts to go north-west to Mysia and Bithynia towards the Black Sea, but the Holy Spirit prevented Paul and his team. So they had to follow the road until it ended, and the road ended by the sea at the coastal city of Troas. This is where Paul and his companions found themselves.

Finding Yourself at Troas

About two years ago while I was Rector of St Thomas', Crookes, in Sheffield, it began to become clear to me that, as I was going about the Lord's business, he was saying something to me that was quite unexpected: the team I had been training up were now ready to take over, so I should give it to them. I talked about it with the team and they agreed—which made me feel somewhat surplus to requirement! But it was clearly the right thing to do. My role, in relation to these other leaders, was to change from being the leader of the church to being more of a spiritual 'father.' (Paul himself comments to the Corinthians that 'you have many teachers but not many fathers,' 1 Cor 4.15.) Our commitment to mission had led to the establishment of the Order of Mission, and I have been appointed 'Superior' of the Order, which simply means taking on that fathering role.

So I found myself, as it were, at Troas and thought that the Lord was obviously calling me to a new thing

At the same moment as these discussions, I was approached by Walt Kallestad, leader of the largest Lutheran congregation in America with a membership of 12,000 people in Phoenix, Arizona. He had come to the conviction that they needed to fundamentally rethink what they were doing, and he had come to Sheffield to find out what has been happening at St Thomas'. Through a series of extraordinary meetings and conversations, he invited me to join the staff there. So I found myself, as it were, at Troas and thought that the Lord was obviously calling me to a new thing.

You may have been in a similar situation yourself. You try one thing, and it does not quite work. So you try another thing, and that does not work either. But because you are about the Lord's business, you just keep on doing the thing that you are clear you need to be doing—fulfilling the Great Commission (Matt 28.19), building the church of Jesus Christ, and teaching them and participating with them on a daily basis. You are engaged in the upward dimension, the inward dimension and the outward dimension that are all part of normal Christian ministry. And as you do that, you find yourself in a particular situation where the Lord reveals to you an opportunity.

And when we find ourselves in this situation, how do we seek to make the right choices?

And when we find ourselves in this situation, working within the sovereignty of God, how do we seek to make the right choices? These are enormous questions for leaders that can have a profound effect on our ministry.

Kairos and Chronos

The first thing is to recognize the *time*. In my situation, it was very clear to me that this was a special time; it was a decisive, if not definitive, moment in my life, a time when I needed to make a decision. It is the kind of time that Jesus describes when he begins his ministry, as recorded in Mark 1.15:

'The time is right.'

In the text of Mark the word used is not *chronos* but *kairos*. *Chronos* describes the day-to-day experience that all of us have of time passing. But *kairos* describes the in-breaking of God to shake us from our chronological experience, a moment to make us sit up and take notice.

In reality, we have lots of little *kairos* moments throughout the day; like speed bumps on the road, they make us stop and check and reflect on what we are doing. But most of the time, in response to these, we just keep on going. In theory, speed bumps are there to make us go slower. But most of us try to find the speed which would enable the speed bump to affect us least! When God is trying to get our attention, very often we continue with what we are doing at such a speed that the interruption has as little impact on us as possible. But there come moments when we find ourselves at Troas, and the speed bump is so big that we cannot ignore it.

Exercise

If we begin to identify these little *kairos* moments, then we will be better able to recognize the *kairos* times that really are definitive in our lives when they come to us.

So spend a few moments now reflecting: when did you last have a *kairos* moment today? It may be as a result of something you read, or something someone said to you; it may have come from an encounter, perhaps someone really irritating you. What did you do with this moment?

When we recognize such times as *kairos* moments, we are recognizing that this is a moment for the breaking in of the kingdom of God. Jesus went on to say (in Mark 1.15) '…the kingdom of God is at hand'; it is very, very near. Through this membrane between the *current* world and the *coming* world there is now a thin place and the kingdom is easily grasped. It is not a long distance from where you are to where you need to be, and the way you get there, says Jesus, is to repent and believe, to go through an inner change and be actively pursuing the faith that God calls you to put into practice.

Step 2: Form a Team

For almost every Christian, there is at least one person looking to us for an example, and so we all have some sort of leadership responsibility. (Everyone looks like a sheep from in front, and a shepherd from behind!) When we have recognized a time, a *kairos* moment, what should we do to exercise our leadership? We return to Paul as the story continues in Acts 16.9–10:

> During the night Paul had a vision of a man of Macedonia standing and begging him, 'Come over to Macedonia and help us.' After Paul had seen the vision, we got ready at once to leave for Macedonia, concluding that God had called us to preach the gospel to them.

This is the beginning of a section in Acts known as the 'we' passages, where Luke moves from being a careful historian (as he describes himself at the beginning of his gospel) to being a vital eye witness. Paul knows that this is a *kairos* moment, since he has had his options narrowed down and found himself at Troas—a city known in Greek as Alexandria, in all likelihood founded by Alexander himself. Whilst there, he has had this vision of a Macedonian, the epitome of which was Alexander himself, calling him to come over and help them. Paul has identified the *time*; now he needs to form a *team*. The vision was given to *him* and yet Luke's account goes on: '…so *we*…' Paul has shared his vision with those around him; having identified the time, he is clear that he needs to form a team.

As a leader, suppose God speaks clearly to you, you have great opportunities, and circumstances come together. Is your next thought: 'Who's in the team?' Usually our answer to this would be 'no.' And yet it is quite clear in Scripture, both in the teaching of Jesus and the experience of the early church, the first thing they thought about once they recognized the time—the opportunity, the moment of the breaking in of God's kingdom—was to form a team.

Now God really, really believes in teams. On the way to Jerusalem, Jesus needed a donkey and so he sent two people. That is a person who believes in teams; he could easily have sent one person, but he sent two. In fact, in the counsel of Scripture it is an unusual event when God only sends one person. As we see the unfolding story of God's salvation, he is always working in community and through teams. The Old Testament tells us that 'Two are better than one' (Eccl 4.9); you cannot get simpler than that. Human beings are social creatures; we are designed to function in community and we are not going to be very effective otherwise.

So at these *kairos* moments, how do we go about forming a team? Paul clearly did it by sharing his vision, by putting his experience of hearing from God out there for others to hear.

Extraverting our Experiences

There are certain things in following Jesus that are easier for introverts, and there are other things that are easier for extraverts. For example, praying is much easier for introverts because all the material on prayer is written by introverts (at least as far as I can tell). There are other things that are easier for extraverts to do—for example, sharing your experience with others. Just as everyone must learn about praying, even if it does not come naturally, it is equally important that we all learn to 'extravert' our experience, even if this does not come naturally. Scripture usually refers to this as our 'testimony' and (according to Revelation 12.11) there are only two things that overcome the power of our enemy: the blood of the lamb, which is an eternal reality, always present; and the word of our testimony, not just the particular experience of God's power in Jesus but the actual expression of it.

> *'Extraverting'
> our experience is
> tremendously important,
> and it is the way that
> God gathers the team*

So 'extraverting' our experience is tremendously important, and it is the way that God gathers the team. It is the way that God solidifies who it is that he has given you to get on with the task at this special time.

In Phoenix I am known as Minister at Large, which means I will be working with the ministry team, mentoring them and modelling a new kind of ministry, helping them to restructure and to set a new direction. It is a huge challenge, because the whole world has wanted to become like the mega-church movement in America, and here we have a mega-church saying that they think they have missed what it is God wants them to be.

I will be working with the ministry team there—but who is my team in the task to go and work with them? As it turned out, three couples have gone with us, so there are eight adults and six children who have gone to Phoenix. These are people who have heard me talk about my experience of God's guidance, and believe that God is calling them along too. It looks like this is a big job since we have a big team!

Exercise

Think of an area of ministry where you are in a 'time'—it may be within your leadership, in the thing you are leading in your church, in your small group, your ministry, or with your family. For any of these, who is in your team?

More generally, who are the three people who are your closest team members? Most people could name one, but you have to be serious about teams to be able to name three.

Step 3: Identify the Target

You have recognized a time, a *kairos* moment in which God is bringing together something that speaks to your greatest desires and expectations and hopes—even to your ambitions. (It is not an ungodly thing to have ambitions, since these are the things that God puts in us.) You have begun to gather the team; you have a sense of the people who are just wanting to be with you, who are loyal to you and you are loyal to them. (You may not use covenant language in your relationship with them—but you are going to stay together through thick and thin.) There is a whole new area of ministry opening up to you. What do you need to do next? Let us see what Paul did.

> From Troas we put out to sea and sailed straight for Samothrace, and the next day on to Neapolis. From there we travelled to Philippi, a Roman colony and the leading city of that district of Macedonia. And we stayed there several days.

> On the Sabbath we went outside the city gate to the river, where we expected to find a place of prayer. We sat down and began to speak to the women who had gathered there. One of those listening was a woman named Lydia, a dealer in purple cloth from the city of Thyatira, who was a worshipper of God. The Lord opened her heart to respond to Paul's message. When she and the members of her household were baptized, she invited us to her home. 'If you consider me a believer in the Lord,' she said, 'come and stay at my house.' And she persuaded us.
>
> (Acts 16.11–15)

This is the first venture of Paul into Europe—a massive watershed in the story of the spreading of the gospel. Not only is he venturing into Europe for the first time; he is also venturing into a Latin speaking, non-synagogue worshipping Roman colony. So he is (in cultural terms) stepping onto the surface of the moon. Everybody talks another language; there is no place where he can identify with an ethnic group of people who might welcome him; and the city itself is run like a miniature version of Rome—in fact, the literature tells us that it was sometimes called 'Little Rome.' It is a strictly run environment, and was in fact a retirement spot for the Roman Army. Senior officers from the army were given portions of land on retirement from service, so it was a first-century 'Costa Geriatrica.' Such places are generally committed to leisure time, and to spending money and time on leisure.

The Person of Peace
So what did Paul do? He found one person—just one person—who was the identifiable gatekeeper who welcomed him, someone who liked him and could connect with him at more than one level. This person was described for Paul (and for all the rest of us in the church) by Jesus; it is called the 'person of peace.'

> After this the Lord appointed seventy-two others and sent them two by two ahead of him to every town and place where he was about to go. He told them, 'The harvest is plentiful, but the workers are few. Ask the Lord of the harvest, therefore, to send out workers into his harvest field. Go! I am sending you out like lambs among wolves. Do not take a purse or bag or sandals; and do not greet anyone on the road.
>
> 'When you enter a house, first say, "Peace to this house." If a man of peace is there, your peace will rest on him; if not, it will return to you. Stay in that house, eating and drinking whatever they give you, for the worker deserves his wages. Do not move around from house to house'.
>
> (Luke 10.1–5)

Jesus has identified a *time*. It is not ploughing time (which could be hard work) or sowing time (which could be boring) or waiting time (which could be even more boring) but harvest time—which means it is going to be fun! Second, he has formed a *team* of seventy-two. He has given the strategy outlined here to his twelve disciples (see Luke 9), but so as to underline for all time that this is not just for the apostolic band of the first apostles, he finds seventy-two others. Notice that they are just called 'others'—that is, they are ordinary people like me and you. He puts them into thirty-six teams, and sends them out with a very simple and encouraging word:

'You are probably going to get eaten alive. But do not take any defence along with you, and do not take anything that will support you in any material way that you know of. Go completely vulnerable because that way you will be really ready to spot the person I have placed in each environment that I am sending you as the one who will be your person of peace.'

In other words, the third thing he does is to give them a *target*. And they will find their target because this is the person who will support them in their ministry—and they have no other support. So often we gather around ourselves resources and material and emotional support which keep us from seeing how God is already opening up the way for us.

Who is the person of peace for me in Phoenix? It is Walt Kallestad, the pastor of the church in America that I am going to. He has begun opening all sorts of doors for us. Seven years ago we began to pray that an American publisher would contact us to publish the Lifeskills (now Lifeshapes) material we had developed, since an English publisher would probably not have the resources to put behind the project. He has started contacting publishers and persuading them to publish some of the material I teach—all without me doing anything! What we needed is a person of peace to open the door, since American publishers did not know who we were.

Recognizing the Person
But what does this person of peace, this target person, look like? When you enter a house (says Jesus) first say 'Peace to this house' then stay there and do not move around. In other words, a person of peace looks like someone with whom you can have a long-term relationship. When you offer your peace to this person (and mean it) you will notice something about the way this person receives your peace that will create a foundation on which to build relationship. This means that we need to be asking ourselves a question as we meet people for the first time: is there a sense of peacefulness, of opportunity, a sense of openness and welcome on which you could build a relationship? A lot of the time we do not know the answer, because we have never learnt to

look for it. But Jesus says it is the fundamental strategy of all evangelism. It is the fundamental issue of relationship building—which is what evangelism is all about. Evangelism is the kingdom dimension to the normal human process of making friends.

That long-term relationship is expressed by the fact that the person you are now thinking about being your friend is prepared to serve you by sharing their resources with you. 'Stay in that house, eating and drinking whatever they give you.' That is a big deal for a Jew, because what if it is a Gentile that is your person of peace? You are not allowed to cross the threshold—and you are certainly not allowed to eat their food! But Jesus makes no exceptions; whoever is the person of peace that the Holy Spirit has prepared for you, that is the one. And you will recognize them because they like you and they give you stuff—their time, their energy and their money.

Paul's Person in Europe

How does this work for Paul in Acts 16? Here he is in a Latin-speaking Roman city. There is no synagogue, and in fact (we know from archaeology) there will be no synagogue for hundreds of years. Yet this is the place that God has chosen he will have his first church in Europe. So how will Paul tackle this? Recognizing that Jesus is smarter than he is (something we could all do with remembering) he goes back to Jesus' strategy in Luke 10. If we all followed Jesus' strategy we would find our ministry easier, more restful and massively more successful—but most of us want to find more than one person. But Jesus says 'Do not go from house to house.' So Paul finds the one man of peace—though in this case it is a woman. And it looks like a fairly unlikely match, because Lydia runs the first-century equivalent of a fashion house, and Paul probably looks highly unfashionable after all the trials and tribulations of his travels.

Moreover, the idea of Paul and his companions staying at the house of a single woman takes some getting used to—'and she persuaded us…eventually.' (It is not so clear in English, but in the original text there is a good deal of ambivalence suggested.) This is so against the cultural norms of the day that it would be unthinkable, and yet she was able to persuade them. How was this possible? Because they were looking for her, and were expecting her (if she was their person of peace) to invite them to her home—because that is what Jesus said would happen.

The Quest for Success

If Christians would only follow this simple strategy, it would be amazing how much more fruit and breakthrough we would see. Instead, we get captured by the crowd, we get dazzled by the opportunity for success. It is usually success that stops fruitfulness more than difficulty. I have seen a lot of examples of that in my own life, where I have seen immediate, surprising success which has stopped the real fruit because I get crowd-conscious instead of being person-oriented.

So we continually need to ask: who is God's person for me? It is around this person that God will organize his kingdom activities. Suppose you are trying to start small groups, or an Alpha course, in your church. Usually we try to convince everybody, but that never works because it simply cannot be done. We will never get everyone to agree. So we end up convincing some but then are left with the angry brigade who will never be convinced. And the only thing we have succeeded in doing is creating division. What would be a lot better would be to say 'I think it is time for us to do a whole new thing, and I am just going to ask God to give me a team and I am then going to target one person who will lead on this.'

Another way of thinking about this is through Jesus' teaching that the kingdom of heaven is like the leaven in the dough (Matt 13.33). Here, and in some of the other kingdom parables, Jesus is telling us that kingdom things start small but end up having a great effect. If you want to start small groups, just start one, because if it is a good one, it will multiply—and you will have two. And if they are good ones they will multiply and then you will have four. And then the other people, who would have been against you if you had tried to persuade them, will be convinced. Because the one thing that convinces nay-sayers more than anything else is fruitfulness. It is always fruitfulness that silences criticism and opposition. The same is true if you are wanting to start Alpha; ask yourself who is really keen? You do not need a lot of people—only one.

This might all seem like a strange strategy to us because we are used to trying to deal with the crowd. But it is the only strategy that Jesus offers and it is the one that he himself practices. As his ministry becomes well-known, people are beginning to coalesce around him and wanting to spend time with him. But Jesus is looking for that one person, his person of peace. When he spots Peter he says to him: 'You're it!' And note what happens next. Jesus stays in his home and this place then becomes his headquarters and the base for all his activity in the region of Galilee. Similarly, when he was down in Judea, his man of peace was Lazarus and his ministry there appears to have been based in Lazarus' home.

Exercise

Think about a situation that you are in—a time of difficulty or a time of opportunity—and you will by now have thought about the team. The next question is, who is your person of peace?

Again and Again...and Again

Let us return to Paul and his companions. They are on a long journey from Troas via Samothrace to Neapolis and then on to Philippi. We are not sure whether they went by land or by boat—you can do either. Paul knows it is the time, he has his team, so what is he praying for during the journey? Well, of course he is praying for his person of peace, his target. And he finds his person of peace and starts a church in her house. (I apologise to those who do not believe in women's ministry; it is a bit inconvenient that the first church in Europe is led by a woman.) But once he had done that, the amazing thing is that he does the same again.

We read in Acts 16.16f that Paul and his friends are being followed and yelled at by a so-called prophetess, a slave girl possessed by a demon described in the original as a 'Python spirit,' which was associated with the Oracle of Delphi. (This is glossed over by English versions, but for a good exposition of this, see Peter Wagner's commentary on Acts). Eventually Paul gets fed up with this happening every day, so he turns to the slave girl and effectively says 'Buzz off!' and the demon does. Then all hell breaks loose—literally. The slave owners realise they are in trouble, since the girl does not have the spirit any more, and they drag Paul and his companions to the magistrate's court. They get out the rods, the bundles of sticks (called 'fasces' which is where we get our word 'Fascist' from) and give them a good beating before throwing them in prison. And through all this, Paul finds his second person of peace.

The prison is a cave, a single room with bars in front of it, and most likely there is a niche at the back where they shackle the most dangerous prisoners. It is probably also the place in the cave where all the prisoners relieve themselves. This is where Paul and Silas, beaten and bloody, are chained to the wall. At around midnight, they are singing choruses and of course all the other prisoners, who are in the same room, are listening to them as are all the guards. And in response to Paul and Silas' praise, there is an earthquake; the bars fall away, and the warder assumes all the prisoners have escaped, so rather than being killed slowly by crucifixion he decides to kill himself quickly. But Paul stops him and shows that they are all there. The warder responds by asking what he must to do be saved.

Now if you ever find yourself with someone kneeling in front of you, having laid aside his sword, and asking what he must to do be saved, then I hope you will by now be able to spot that this is a person of peace. So this man becomes a Christian, and his whole household is baptised (now I have to apologise to those who do not believe in infant baptism, since we know that the household comprises at least three generations of different ages) and Paul leaves Philippi with two congregations established. What is more, he leaves with his head held high as a Roman citizen and makes sure the magistrates eat humble pie before he goes. It is a typically Pauline thing to do, and it is exactly what I would have wanted to do in the same situation.

Step 4: Tackle the Task

We have now come to the last part of our strategy for fruitfulness—and it is the simplest one to state. Look again at Jesus' instructions to the 72 in Luke 10. Having identified the time, formed the team and explained their target, he now gives them a *task*:

> 'Tell them the kingdom of God is near. Heal the sick, cleanse the lepers, cast out demons, raise the dead.' (Luke 9.1, 2 and 10.9)

It is just the normal business of the kingdom. And he goes on to say (in Luke 10.16), 'If they accept you, they accept me, and if they accept me, they accept the one who sent me. But if they reject you, then they are rejecting me, and then they are in big trouble. So don't waste your time with them, don't try and persuade them and bring them round to your opinion; shake the dust off your feet and go and look for the person of peace that I have prepared for you.'

If we followed this strategy, our building projects would be easier, our development of ministries would be easier, our strategies for evangelism would be massively easier—because this is the Jesus way. We have it twice, once in the example of Jesus in Luke 10, and once in the experience of Paul as recorded in the eye-witness account of Luke in Acts 16. It is not easy, but it is simple.

One of the most important things I have learned in 21 years of ordained ministry is that life is complicated. And complexity is resolved not by greater complexity, but by simplicity. I look at my brother and sister clergy, my fellow leaders in Christian ministry, and I wonder why they are setting up such complex ways of doing things. As far as I can see, the complexity of their lives would be resolved through some of the simplicity that Jesus offers us. It is not easy, but it is simple.

Exercise

What is the task that God is calling you to now? How can you express it with the kind of simplicity with which Jesus expresses it?

How can this understanding of time, team, target and task help simplify your understanding of the particular ministry God has called you into?

3 Part 2: The Secret of Fruitfulness

We can learn from Paul about the 'outer' aspects of fruitfulness, about fruitful strategy.

But we can also learn from him about the 'inner' aspects of fruitfulness. This is important since good tools do not make a skilful carpenter; good strategies alone do not make for a fruitful life. And this is possible, since we not only have an account of what Paul did (in Acts) but also an account from him of what he thought (in his letters, and in particular, his letters to the church at Corinth). In the same way that Jesus must have shared with his disciples something of his inner struggles and reflections (otherwise we would have no way of knowing about his temptations and wrestling in Gethsemane), so Paul shared his experience not only with his travelling companions, but also with the Christians in Corinth—and so with us as we read his letters.

The Heart of the Matter

The real question concerning the inner life of a leader is this: what needs to happen inside a person for that person to be successful? I am aware that some people have difficulty with using the language of 'success' in relation to ministry—in fact, in many ways I am reluctant to use that language myself. But we are called by God in creation to be fruitful, and (Jesus tells us) we are called in redemption by our Father to be *very* fruitful.

We are called to be fruitful, both in the procreative sense and in the general sense, in our creation. In the first chapter of the Bible, God simply says, 'Be fruitful' (Gen 1.28). In our redemption, as part of the new creation, Jesus says to us in his last parable as part of his final discourse, 'You have been called and appointed to bear *much* fruit' (see John 15.5). This is not an alternative way of being a Christian, it is not something for the special few, for those who are most gifted or skilled or talented—this is for everybody.

This is not an alternative way of being a Christian, it is not something for the special few

So perhaps we can put the question this way: what is it that needs to happen to enable us to be fruitful? One thing is clear: fruitfulness means multiplication. It is no good an apple tree producing apples, but none of them ever becoming new apple trees.

What is important about fruit is not whether it looks attractive, smells nice or tastes good. These ideas may be important, but at the very best they are only secondary. The primary purpose of fruit is to multiply that which it is the fruit of.

Exercise

Reflect on your experience of Christian living and ministry to date. What have been the things in you that have led to fruitfulness?

The Context of Corinth

In order to begin exploring this question, we are going to look at Luke's account of Paul's ministry in Corinth, in Acts 18. As we explore this and expand some of the details, it will give us some important background, so that when we read some of Paul's own testimony in 1 and 2 Corinthians, we will understand a little more of what he was trying to say.

> After this, Paul left Athens and went to Corinth. There he met a Jew named Aquila, a native of Pontus, who had recently come from Italy with his wife Priscilla, because Claudius had ordered all the Jews to leave Rome. Paul went to see them, and because he was a tentmaker as they were, he stayed and worked with them. Every Sabbath he reasoned in the synagogue, trying to persuade Jews and Greeks.
>
> When Silas and Timothy came from Macedonia, Paul devoted himself exclusively to preaching, testifying to the Jews that Jesus was the Christ. But when the Jews opposed Paul and became abusive, he shook out his clothes in protest and said to them, 'Your blood be on your own heads! I am clear of my responsibility. From now on I will go to the Gentiles.'
>
> Then Paul left the synagogue and went next door to the house of Titius Justus, a worshipper of God. Crispus, the synagogue ruler, and his entire household believed in the Lord; and many of the Corinthians who heard him believed and were baptized. (Acts 18.1–6)

Paul, on his way through Greece, has now reached the ancient home of the Spartans—Corinth, on the peninsula in the south of Greece, and one of the great cities of the world. Like the other cities of Ephesus (which he will soon visit), Rome and Alexandria, it is a place which both calls to the world and speaks to the world. Near to Corinth is another city, Cenchreae. Today they are separated by a large canal, but in Paul's day the ships which arrived in Corinth would be unloaded by slaves and then dragged by hand across the short distance of the land bridge, to be put in the water again at the other port. The same would happen in reverse for ships travelling in the other direction. Although this was a lot of work, it saved the ships sailing round the peninsula. As a result, Corinth was at one of the naval crossroads of the world. It was probably one of the first cities to be a free port; it was the place everyone went for anything that was new.

Paul's People in Exile

In AD 49 the Jews were expelled from Rome by Claudius, possibly because of riots caused by Christians preaching the gospel (see Suetonius' Life of Claudius 25.4). Twenty thousand of them had to find a new home, and one of the places that they went to was Corinth. It was on a principal trade route, and so when many of them reached there on their travels, they stayed. When Paul arrived, he found a city teaming with people and a hinterland surrounding the city made up of shanty towns and people living in the open air. And, by and large, these people were his own people. Eventually the Jews were allowed to return to Rome, but in the meantime they were homeless. Among them were a couple called Aquila and Priscilla, part of this exiled people group ejected from Rome. Aquila and Priscilla are already Christians and they are tentmakers, which means they are in the number one new industry for Corinth—there were thousands of people wanting a tent! You can imagine the scene: you arrive in the new city; there is nowhere to stay; so the first thing you do is to look for a tentmaker. Paul, too, is a tentmaker, and so they have much in common.

From the account in Acts 18, it is apparent that Paul only has the Sabbath on which to conduct his ministry. During the week he is supporting himself with his tentmaking—but he is also supporting his own people, the Jews, by means of the production of tents, along with Priscilla and Aquila.

The Gift for Ministry

When Silas and Timothy come from Macedonia, where they have been supporting and encouraging the church, we are told (in Paul's letters) that they bring a large gift with them from the churches in Macedonia and in particular from Philippi. Philippi (as we have seen) was a wealthy city, even though the churches in Macedonia probably were not, and this gift means that Paul no longer has to work. So we see in Acts 18.5 that when Silas and Timothy arrive, Paul can 'devote himself exclusively to preaching.' From the text of his letters it is quite clear that the gift released him into the ministry that he wanted to get on with—because there was a huge harvest to be had in this city. The harvest was being ripened by the social factors that usually condition revival—social factors of community brokenness. In verse 10 the Lord says unequivocally to Paul that there are many people in the city that he is going to call to himself. And by the time that Paul leaves Corinth to continue his ministry in Ephesus, on his way to make good his vows in Jerusalem, there are probably thousands of people in this newly planted church.

The harvest was being ripened by the social factors that usually condition revival

Paul's Pattern of Ministry

In his own inimitable style, Paul continues to preach in the synagogue, to the god-fearers and the ethnic Jews, and eventually they reach the point where they do not want to listen any more. So Paul shakes the dust out of his clothes (v 6), the standard way in which a rabbi would indicate that he is no longer going to talk to them. It would say to them, 'You are like the pagan nations,' for when a Jews came back to the land of Israel, they would shake the dust out of their clothes so as not to contaminate the land of blessing. So shaking the dust out of your clothes is like saying to someone, 'Clearly you are not under the blessing of God; I am going to go and find out where it is.' Here, Paul is doing this in the opposite way to the way you would expect; he is now going to go to the gentiles.

When he left the synagogue, he set up shop next door. But not only has he set up next door—he has taken the vicar with him! We read (v 8) that Crispus, the synagogue ruler, and his whole household—his wife, children, his slaves, everyone who is part of the household—goes next door with Paul.

It is like saying to someone, 'Clearly you are not under the blessing of God; I am going to go and find out where it is'

So Sosthenes is left trying to run a church with Paul as his neighbour; it is hard to imagine how difficult that must have been! And the Jews, probably with the help of others who had opposed Paul in Macedonia, back in Thessalonica, put together a case, and when the governor was hearing cases they came before him at the magistrate's court. But it did not quite go the way they expected—it rather backfired on them. Gallio, whom we know from other sources and from archaeology was the governor of Achaia at that time and sat as a magistrate in Corinth, decided that this matter was about religion. He was more interested in whether or not your chariot was speeding and suchlike—so he told them to leave the court. They were so incensed at the lack of interest by the authorities that they turned on the (new) synagogue ruler, Sosthenes, and beat him up.

This whole episode was, no doubt, instrumental in a life-changing experience for Sosthenes. Paul's first letter to the Corinthians was written from Ephesus about two years later. Paul had left Priscilla and Aquila there, gone to Jerusalem to fulfil his vows, visited his home church of Antioch, and then returned to Ephesus through Galatia and Phrygia. Whilst there, a small delegation of leaders from the church in Corinth had come to him to explain some of the difficulties they were facing. They returned with the letter—which begins: 'Paul, called to be an apostle, and our brother Sosthenes.' Not only has he become a Christian, but he is now one of the leaders in the church and becomes co-writer of the letter with Paul.

Paul's Fruitfulness

All this is important by way of setting the scene for thinking about fruitfulness, since Paul clearly had a fruitful ministry in Corinth. It is obvious that there are problems in the Corinthian church, but my guess is that most people in ministry would live with them if they had a church like the one at Corinth. There are thousands of members, they are transforming the city and drawing in all kinds of people—which is probably why it is such a hothouse (or some would say nuthouse).

But listen to what Paul says about all this: 'For the message of the cross is foolishness to those who are perishing, but to us who are being saved, it is the power of God' (1 Cor 1.18). He goes on explain what this meant for him in his preaching at Corinth:

> When I came to you, brothers, I did not come with eloquence or superior wisdom as I proclaimed to you the testimony about God. For I resolved to know nothing while I was with you except Jesus Christ and him crucified. I came to you in weakness and fear and with much trembling. My message and my preaching were not with wise and persuasive words, but with a demonstration of the Spirit's power, so that your faith might not rest on men's wisdom, but on God's power.
>
> (1 Cor 2.1–5)

So having looked at the context, let us now look at the content of Paul's message. And the content of his message is the cross of Christ, lived out and modelled in the life of Paul. It is what he said, but it is also what he did; it is what he shared in his preaching, but it is also what he represented in his living. Whilst he was in Corinth, he had suffered attacks, but he had been promised by the Lord that on this occasion the attacks would not result in physical harm. He had already suffered great physical harm before he had arrived in Corinth, and indeed he was going to suffer much more through the rest of his life. This had been prophesied about him; at the moment of his conversion the Lord had said to Ananias 'He is going to have to suffer a lot in order to do all the things that I am going to call him to do.'

Paul's Request

But by the time of this Corinthian expedition, it seems as though Paul had reached the point of wanting all this opposition to stop. A group of Pharisaic teachers were following him around to each place that he went, trying to destroy the churches that he had planted, and trying to destroy the work that he had established. These are the people that I believe he describes in 2 Cor 12 as his 'thorn in the flesh.' There are lots of theories about the meaning of this term, but my theory is simply this: Paul was a man of the Bible, and if he uses a phrase from the Bible, he probably means what that phrase means in the Bible. 'Thorn in the flesh' means people who are a pain in the neck; it is Old Testament imagery of what the people in the land of Canaan would become if they were not expelled from the land (see Num 33.55). So it is nothing to do with sickness or eyesight or anything like that—it is people, problem people who are giving him a hard time.

It is absolutely devastating in its effect if we are prepared to allow it to settle in our hearts

So Paul shaves all the hair off his body, puts it in a bag, and takes it to Jerusalem (I know it sounds a bit weird, but that is the way people took vows in those days). Having taken this Nazirite-vow-in-reverse, what he has to do is put the hair in the fires of the altar and then make his request of the Lord. My belief is that this occasion, in Jerusalem before the altar, is when he 'asked the Lord three times' to take this away (2 Cor 12). But the Lord said something that I have taken to be one of my life Scriptures. It is fairly unequivocal, and it is absolutely devastating in its effect if we are prepared to allow it to settle in our hearts:

> My grace is sufficient for you, says the Lord, for my power is made perfect in weakness (2 Cor 12.9).

The key to fruitfulness is weakness. And we need to get hold of this truth, because we need to be fruitful. I think that Paul's testimony is so important that the Holy Spirit saw fit to make sure that it was enshrined within Scripture for all time. Weakness is the key.

Weakness is the Key

It was not just true for Paul; it was also true for Sosthenes. What would be the effect on someone of being beaten up in Gallio's courtroom? It is difficult to say for certain. But it is clear that it was a step on the way to Sosthenes becoming co-author of one the most important letters in the New Testament. And it was true for the city of Corinth. As it was inundated with Jewish refugees, the over-strained infrastructure became ripe and ready for God's powerful work in bringing in a harvest.

This is not a novel idea, but it is the message, the ministry and the mentoring approach of Jesus. Jesus began his ministry with these words (according to Mark); 'The time is right, the kingdom of God is at hand; repent and believe the good news.' Now, how do you enter the kingdom? The time is right, the kingdom is at hand, it is right here and now—but there are preconditions to entering it. These pre-conditions are *metanoia* and *pistis*—that we repent and believe. Another way of expressing this is that the pre-conditions for entering the kingdom are death and life; in the life of Jesus the pre-conditions for the new things are the cross and resurrection. The pre-conditions for discipleship are: take up your cross, do not attempt to preserve your life but give it up, and follow me.

Do not attempt to preserve your life but give it up and follow me

Weakness and Victory

So the pre-condition for fruitfulness—which come from the fountainhead of cross and resurrection, that flow out of an empty grave—is the same thing, weakness. It feels like death, it feels horrible, unpleasant, like pressure, stress, persecution, brokenness. So does that mean that we are simply to feel miserable? It cannot be this, since Paul is the same person who says that we are more than conquerors, that we are not victims but victors, that nothing can separate us from the love of God. He is the one that wrote all those triumphant passages in the New Testament, who says that we have available to us more than we can ever imagine. So clearly Paul does not want us to be miserable!

Before exploring what this means, I should make it clear that I am sharing my testimony. In my own experience and ministry, this is the basis of any fruitfulness that I have seen. I am not wanting to measure one person's fruitfulness against another's—when we get to heaven, I suspect we will find that there are many whose names we do not even know who are way ahead of us in fruitfulness. I always remember the story of Whitfield who had some theological differences with Wesley. (In fact they continued in fellowship; it was often their followers who had more problems with each other.) Once, some of Whitfield's followers asked him: 'Do you think we will see Wesley in glory?' to which

Whitfield replied: 'I fear not, for he will be so near the eternal throne and we at such a distance, we shall hardly get sight of him.' (See *Wycliffe Handbook of Preaching and Preachers*, W Wiersbe, Moody Press, 1984, p 255.)

But to the extent to which I have seen fruitfulness in my own life, I have to say that this has been the basis of it. It is weakness and brokenness; it is not being skilled or talented or clever or 'anointed'—it is none of those things. It is being broken and weak and not being good—and not feeling very good. We learn the basic exchange that needs to take place: as we give to God our brokenness, he gives to us his wholeness. As we give to him our weakness, he gives to us his power. As we give to him our death and our experience of death, he gives to us his life. As Jesus says 'Father, into your hands I commit my Spirit' (Luke 23.46), so the Father honours his Son by raising him from the dead and setting him in the highest place above every name.

The Key Question

So the most important question about our weakness is not '*Why* do I feel weak?' (that is a question you can discuss with a counsellor at some point) but '*Where* do I feel weak?'

- Do you have a tendency to sin? If you do not, then you are an angelic interloper and you will be found out! Yes, you do, and you probably have what Wesley called a 'darling sin,' a pet sin that you nurture.

- Do you have things about you that continually make you feel less of the person that you want to be? Things that continually pop up in the most inconvenient moments—when you are about to preach, or share God's love with someone, or when you are returning home to your family and want to be everything you can for them?

- Do you have a sense that you are misunderstood, misrepresented or marginalized? That this misunderstanding means you feel estranged from those you want to be close to?

It is in these areas that God will bring his fruitfulness.

Revival—Starting with Me

This truth is not just relevant to us as individuals either; it also relates to the question of 'corporate revival.' By this I mean a sustained visitation of God that transforms community after community. It is often written about, discussed and debated. It is a relatively rare phenomenon, but it has been a historical reality for this nation; the last time it occurred was probably the Hebridean revival of 1948–52, and before that the Welsh revival of 1904. For a large-scale revival we would need to look at Azusa Street revival of 1906 which led to the Pentecostal movement, probably the largest movement of humanity of any kind over the last couple of hundred years. Other revival movements have taken place in Latin America, in Argentina and more latterly in Columbia, and Nigeria is a contemporary revival 'hot-spot.'

What has to happen before revival comes? Prayer is essential for revival—but we have been praying for it for over twenty years. Unity is important, but the church in Britain is probably more unified than any church in the Western world—far more than any other church I have visited. The Evangelical Alliance has produced a level of ecumenical unity beyond the wildest dreams of places where revival has happened. Of course there is more we can do in these two areas—but are there other pre-conditions we have not yet spotted?

There is much discussion about the pre-conditions for revival, and yet very little talk of corporate brokenness

There is much discussion about the pre-conditions for revival, and yet very little talk of corporate brokenness. But in all my years of study of revivals, the pre-condition of all pre-conditions, as far as I can see, is corporate brokenness. This is true in all the examples I have mentioned. For example, eighteenth-century Britain was an awful place to live for ordinary people to live. And on the geo-political stage it was a time of great anxiety. It was the time when America decided to be independent, when the French Revolution was taking place and there was fear that it was going to come to Britain too. It was a time of massive insecurity. The same becomes clear when you consider the levels of poverty that were commonplace in Wales at the time of the Welsh Revival. And the same is true of the levels of corporate anxiety in Azusa Street, when many thought California was under the judgement of God as a result of the San Francisco earthquake which had just taken place earlier that year. Almost all the accounts of the Argentinian revival mention the failure of Argentina to hold the Falklands as the trigger to corporate revival because the country was so broken about their defeat.

When I have spoken to leaders of the Nigerian revival, interestingly they are ambivalent about the emergence of a more godly government. You would think that they would be glad about this and see it as an answer to prayer. But one of them

'We are not sure we want things to get better until we see the full harvest come in'

said to me: 'yes, we are pleased, and God wanted to do it. But when we were suffering so much, we saw thousands come to Christ, and we are not sure we want things to get better until we see the full harvest come in.'

Living with Brokenness

Paul says, 'I came to you in weakness, I shared with you a message without eloquence and without human wisdom, a simple message of a man nailed to a cross, and I lived the life of one who is crucified'—and you know the effect of this. And in his next letter he articulates the testimony in which God says, 'and that is the way it is always going to be.'

So, how do we live this out and stay sane? How is this emotionally, psychologically and socially sustainable? We cannot all be falling apart from brokenness all the time—so how can we make this work? I believe that it

We cannot all be falling apart from brokenness all the time—so how can we make this work?

works along the lines that Paul himself sets out. He talks about 'boasting' in his weakness, which essentially means articulating what it is. And to articulate your weakness, you first have to identify your weakness. So you have to identify your weakness, articulate it, and then say 'This is me.' And who do you say that to? First, you say it to God, and then you say it to everyone else.

Imagine that I am holding an earthenware pot, that has been broken, but I am holding all the pieces together. If I am holding it well, then at first you might not realize that it is broken at all. It is only if I move my hands that you can see how broken it really is. Watchman Nee (who taught something similar to this) was once asked by one of his students whether he needed to remain broken all the time. After all, he did not want to be miserable; he wanted to enjoy himself too! In reply, Watchman Nee took a biscuit from the table, and broke it and then put the two pieces back together in his hand. He asked the student whether he could see the break, or even guess where the break might be. The student said he could not. Then he asked the student to touch the biscuit, and with the lightest of touches the break became visible.

Held by God

So once we have identified our areas of weakness, of brokenness, the areas where we are not able to do whatever it is we should be doing, we then place that broken piece in the hand of God and say to him: 'Would you hold this for me for the day of healing?' And in God's hand we then become sensitive to the merest touch of his Spirit, because we are conscious not that we are whole, but that we are broken on the way to being whole. We are not conscious that we are powerful, but that we are weak and in the midst of our weakness God is pouring out his power. In his hands, the broken pieces that we are always trying to hide or scramble together and pretend that they are not broken form a container. As it is added to by the pieces that you identify, the earthenware pot in God's hands become larger and larger. And so God is able to pour out a greater anointing on the person who hands to him the most broken pieces. That is why it is the most broken people who are the most anointed. And the least broken people are the least anointed, because God has fewer pieces in his hand to fill.

So do you have a tendency to sin? Do you have an area of your life where, given freedom, you would develop a life-controlling habit or an addiction of some kind or another? Now, counselling is important in these areas, since counselling helps to identify our brokenness. If you have a stone in your shoe, find it—do not just walk around with it in your shoe! But the danger is that counselling does not always help us to take the stone out; in fact, sometimes counselling might even tell us that the stone does not matter, since this is just the way we are. But these things do matter. The right way to deal with them is to say that they matter so much that I am going to take captive every thought and submit it to Christ. I am going to take my

> *I am going to take my little piece of brokenness and I am going to put it into the hands of someone who cares about me*

little piece of brokenness and I am going to put it into the hands of someone who cares about me. And in his hands he will fit it together with the other pieces. And then he fills that piece of brokenness, and the other pieces that he had in his hands, with his anointing power. That is why the most broken people can sometimes look the most complete—not that they are complete, but that in his hands they are complete.

The Key to Fruitfulness
So, to return to the question that we began this section with, what is the key to fruitfulness? Failure. What is the key to wholeness? Brokenness. What is the key to power? Weakness.

Now for many of us this presents a serious problem. All too often we think that ministry is all about being full, but it is not—it is about being empty. When we ask God to fill us, then he does—of course he does, because he loves us. But if we have only give him a few of our broken pieces, if we have only given him a quarter of the broken pot, then he cannot fill us any further. In fact, he longs that we should give him more of the pieces to hold so that he had a bigger container to fill.

We can so easily misunderstand the secret of success; we can so easily misunderstand the fundamentals of fruitfulness. Because it is how much of your brokenness God has in his hands that dictates how much he is able to fill our lives.

From Failure to Fruitfulness

This brokenness need not simply relate to sin; it can also concern simple human weakness. I was born with a funny brain; it is now called 'having dyslexia.' But they did not call it that then; they just called me 'stupid.' And I knew I was not stupid, but I came at the bottom of the class, and examinations cannot lie, can they? What do you do with something like that when you come to Christ? You say to God: 'This is what I am like. I wish I wasn't, so I am not going to pretend that I am glad about it, because I am not. But I am going to put it into your hands, and see what you can do with it.' And God says 'You are probably very good at listening and at verbal communication, so I will make you a preacher and you can tell people stories.' And the same can be true for you with your weaknesses. The key question as to how it is used is: whose hands is it in?

Do you feel left on the edge of things, like an outsider looking in? Do you feel not very clever? Do you feel not very equipped for something you are facing? Whatever it is, is it in your hands or is it in his? Whatever you feel weak about, you can place it in his wounded hands. And when you do that, he takes that piece and the other pieces, and he says to you: 'I will fill this and, if you allow me, I will pour it out. And the pouring out will be greater because the filling up is greater, and the filling up is greater because I have more pieces in my hands.'

4 Conclusion: Lifeshapes

Some of the key principles here—identifying the kairos moment, knowing your person of peace, finding fruitfulness through brokenness—are expressed in the Lifeshapes course.

For the last ten years, Lifeshapes (formerly Lifeskills) has undergirded the mission and ministry of St Thomas', Crookes. Lifeshapes is 'the language of life and leadership,' providing simple values in our post-modern, urban world.

Now Lifeshapes is being published for the first time. Cook Publications is working with Mike Breen and Walt Kallestad (Pastor of the Community Church of Joy, Arizona) to produce a range of resources to enable churches to use the Lifeshapes principles for themselves. The first two publications, *The Passionate Church* and *A Passionate Life* have just been published. These books are an introduction to Lifeshapes for church leaders and members, focussing on life and leadership the way Jesus did it.

The Passionate Church and *A Passionate Life* are the first products in what will eventually form a comprehensive resource for churches worldwide seeking simple ways to help their people grow in their faith and discipleship. The books are supported by the new Lifeshapes website (www.lifeshapes.com) and by an increasing number of Lifeshapes training days and conferences. *The Passionate Church* explains Lifeshapes for church leaders seeking to understand the principles and apply them to their context. *A Passionate Life* is for church members wanting to live discipled lives in the ways that Jesus taught. Both books explain the eight Lifeshapes, which cover a range of Jesus' teaching and offer simple principles to growth in faith.

In the UK, St Thomas' will continue to provide Lifeshapes training and consultancy. *The Passionate Church* and *A Passionate Life* are available exclusively in the UK on our sister site, www.stream247.com. There, you can also find other teaching materials by Mike Breen and register at Lifeshapes conferences, the first of which is in October 2005.